Emotional Recovery from an Affair

How you both move forward

By Richard Schwindt M.S.W., R.S.W.

So the great affair is over so whoever would have guessed
it would leave us so vacant and so deeply unimpressed
It's like our visit to the moon or to that other star
I guess you go for nothing if you really go that far.
Leonard Cohen

Table of Contents

Preface

This book is an emergency guide for the marital crisis that follows the discovery or disclosure of infidelity. It is written for the spouse who cheated and the spouse who was betrayed. Depending on circumstances this may end your marriage but it doesn't have to. While my bias and intention is to save your marriage it is a personal choice only you can make. If it is clear that your marriage is going to end or the affair is going to continue then you might be better off looking at a guide to separation. Keep that in mind when reading the First Aid directions. This is for the couple I see in my office saying: "Help us!"

This is a genuine emotional crisis that carries the risk in some of harm to self and others, and emotional injury which will have to be managed in a climate of pain and distrust. However awful it sounds many couples go through this and come out stronger than they were before. The First Aid directives are meant for immediate guidance. Here is a summary:

Take care of your physical health

Under great stress people let go of basic personal care. This means you need to eat and sleep well, hydrate and exercise. It also means moderation in the use of substances.

Control your emotions

More than anything else I see in my office infidelity and its responses are driven by intense and primitive emotions. These emotions must be managed if you are going to survive the crisis.

The affair ends now

This means everything; all contact, texts, email, calls and involvement. This can be a challenge, particularly when both parties share a workplace.

Get some help

This can take a few forms, including reading the literature on infidelity or seeing a counselor. Having someone objective and knowledgeable is important while emotions are out of control, or if you are having violent or suicidal thoughts.

No rash actions

Decisions to walk out, confront the other party or put the house on the market will likely end badly. You are not at your best right now, and any decisions you make will be distorted by extreme emotion.

Allow yourselves time

Psychological blows take time to heal. They cannot be rushed. This is not going to be better in four weeks or even four months. It may get better then worse again.

The person who had the affair takes responsibility for the affair

Maybe you were having marital and/or sexual problems and maybe they will have to be addressed. That never excuses an affair and doesn't matter in the short run. If the person who had the affair does not take full responsibility, then the marriage will not recover.

The person who cheated enters a period of transparency

This means openness with texts and emails, reporting contact with the other party and frequent contact during absence from home such as business travel.

There is never a reason for abusive behavior

There's going to be anger and rage that needs to be expressed. Deep and powerful emotions that feel (but are not) out of control. Abuse and degradation will wound not heal and could add legal trouble to an already volatile situation.

Be careful with whom you share this information

People who find out about the affair will always remember. I am not saying to tell no one but think through the implications of telling certain people.

Introduction

I think you still love me, but we can't escape the fact that I'm not enough for you. I knew this was going to happen. So I'm not blaming you for falling in love with another woman. I'm not angry, either. I should be, but I'm not. I just feel pain. A lot of pain. I thought I could imagine how much this would hurt, but I was wrong."
Haruki Murakami, South of the Border,
West of the Sun

I go to meet a new couple and find two unhappy looking people in the waiting room. One might be looking tired, confused and angry, and the other may look shamed and furtive. They are in emotional pain and even though one of them is responsible for creating this pain they both deserve my attention and compassion. They are not coming to my office for judgement but to be helped.

Claire looked like she hadn't slept in a week. Her husband hovered over her unsure whether to offer her physical comfort, flee or cry himself...

I have one of the most challenging tasks for a therapist ahead. Every clinician needs to build rapport, soothe ragged emotions, take history, and establish intentions and short term goals in that first hour. We're used to it; it's what we do. And many therapists (including me) will tell you that working with couples is the most difficult thing they do.

The couple in your office following the disclosure of an affair are poised on a knife edge, between fear (loss of love and marriage), guilt (looking at, and seeing the consequences of their actions), anger (our unconscious mind's instinctual protective response) and sadness (loss of innocence and love).

I often tell my clients of the respect I have for their choice to share the most painful things in their life, but I rarely fail to tell couples who come to talk about an affair. Their pain is too blatant and I consider their presence in my office an act of courage. I am more directive to them than other clients because crisis situations call for directive approaches.

In addition, I have to ensure that the person who has been cheated on believes that I understand their dilemma. The cheater is often prepared to do anything they can to make amends and have already discovered that their spouse is far beyond superficial apologies. I have to assess mental status because they are at emotional risk as well.

I have seen everyone in the drama of infidelity. I have seen you after you were caught and before. I have met the person you cheated with. I have worked with the wife of the man who slept with your wife. She didn't know what was happening but felt confused and alone for no reason she could put her finger on. I've seen your kids when they become anxious and stressed. I have seen your adult kids filled with rage and hurt.

This provides me with invaluable perspective. I have also been involved when someone stepped out of their heterosexual marriage with a same sex partner and a same sex marriage when someone stepped out with an opposite sex partner.

Many of my clients move on to renew their marriage and become stronger together; no matter how unlikely that seems at the time of crisis. In this book I have a few agendas. One is the First Aid. I will elaborate on the points above as well as describing the basic dynamics of infidelity and what typically takes place after the disclosure. Secondly, I want to talk about how couples renew their marriage after the shock passes.

This is not a long book. It is not intended as an academic dissertation on infidelity in Western culture. I am a therapist with a private practise. My work is short term. Moreover, people in crisis don't have much patience or ability to read something long winded. They need help now. That said, there are some excellent books on the topic of infidelity noted at the end.

I will be adding some case studies along the way. I am a fiction writer as well as a therapist so while these vignettes may seem to be about my clients they are not. They reflect common experiences shared by thousands of couples.

Be aware that I have a sense of humour that cannot always be repressed. If it sneaks into the text it's not because I do not regard the issues as serious. It is typically me trying not to take myself too seriously. And I don't want to bore you to death with sanctimony. We are complex and sensual creatures. We struggle. We do our best to make amends and become better people.

Why is an affair so emotionally devastating?

These are our lives. You went and broke our lives. You are so much worse than a cheater. You killed something. And you killed it when its back was turned.
David Levithan, The Lover's Dictionary

No matter how challenging or distant your marriage seems the bond runs deep. Affairs can happen in good and bad marriages but either way they are devastating. Our relationship with our spouse becomes normalized over time. He's just there every day. We take out the garbage on Wednesday, curl on Friday and drive the kids to soccer. We have lots of fights or never fight at all. We have great sex or no sex at all.

It becomes so easy to forget the depth and extent that marriage affects every fibre of our being. How good and bad strokes are all forms of emotional engagement. How that distant person remains someone we once loved.

"I don't understand this at all," Sam said, "we've hardly spoken in years, I shouldn't feel the way I feel about her sleeping with another guy."

People bond together in every known society. The rules of this bonding may vary but it is deeply wired within us to form a lasting intimate connection with another. This may be for having children and continuation, as an economic arrangement, companionship or all of these things. No matter why people get together they are wounded by the revelation of infidelity.

Jenny: "I know you feel betrayed."

Rupert: "Well, that's one of the unpleasant side effects of betrayal."

Buffy the Vampire Slayer

Betrayal has the same effect on people, whether they are gay or straight. It is exceedingly rare for someone in a committed relationship of any kind to be okay with cheating.

I see the same kind of devastation in gay and lesbian marriages as I do in heterosexual marriages. However, there is an extra dynamic when someone has an affair with a person who is a different gender than their partner.

Dan and Zachary felt they had a good thing going. When Zachary had an affair with a woman in his office Dan was shocked and confronted him: "Not only are you cheating but you're straight now? Has anything about our relationship been true?"

Devon was devastated when he found out Ellen was having an affair. When he found out that it was with another woman his devastation was overwhelming. He didn't question his wife's sexual orientation so much as his failure as a man.

Someone may be in a marriage or long term relationship with someone who is not the same sexual orientation. That fact is likely not on the table. An affair is still betrayal and more dishonesty. It is not a substitute for living with integrity and being true to yourself.

What is infidelity?

Infidelity is a relationship that invades the boundaries of the primary intimate relationship. This is true whether we are talking marriage, common law marriage or an exclusive relationship. Where this gets sticky is that the definition varies somewhat from person to person. At one of end of the spectrum (an ongoing or long term sexual relationship) everyone can agree that something is wrong. At the other end of the spectrum (an opposite sex friendship) things get tricky and may share a borderland with jealousy.

Sheri and Dylan had been friends since High School. They dated briefly but for many years they had gotten together for drinks once a month to chat and catch up. They had supported each other through many ups and downs. When Sheri married Jack he was still reeling from his divorce. His wife had multiple secret affairs so he told Sheri up front that faithfulness was mandatory if their relationship was going to work. When he found out about her friendship with Dylan he became highly distressed and stopped talking to her.

You can see where this gets difficult; Jack still has to come to terms with past wounds and Sheri doesn't want to lose a lifelong friend.

Alyssa took a call on Sean's cell phone one afternoon while he was golfing. After snooping around for a bit she discovered dozens of texts from his co-worker, Michelle, commenting on his appearance, the great conversations they had together and how much she looked forward to seeing him again. In particular she was looking forward to spending time with him at an out of town conference. After Sean returned Alyssa confronted him demanding to know about his relationship with Michelle. Sean said that it was not physical but that he was not happy with Alyssa and Michelle made him feel good about himself.

So is Sean having an affair? He hadn't previously told Alyssa about his marital dissatisfaction or about his time with Michelle. He really hadn't had sexual contact with Michelle but Alyssa didn't know what to believe.

As you read this you may be triggered. You may read the above and say, "That's not so bad.", or you may say, "Sean is so deceptive." There is an element of interpretation outside of the extremes, as opposed to a precise standard that says this is cheating and this is not.

Maya went to a large conference out of town. During the final banquet people were drinking too much and she ended up having sex with someone she met there. She was devastated afterwards and when she returned home she told her husband, Allen, what had happened then made an appointment to be tested for an STD.

Previously in their relationship Maya has been faithful. However, following this encounter she experienced emotional shock and confessed to Allen. Her devastation, however, was nothing on his. He had no inkling that something like this could happen and broke down emotionally. Maya was consumed by her guilt and a sense of responsibility for his hurt.

Sally was being treated for depression. She had been depressed off and on for years but this time she was in because she had discovered that her husband Curt was sleeping with another woman. This was the third affair that she had found out about and she felt saddened by his need to have another woman in his life. He came to therapy with her and said it was over; from now on he was going to be faithful. He also disclosed to her that he had acquired herpes and now she had to be tested.

This looks like a no brainer; most are going to see Curt as bad news. But that is not how Sally sees him.

Sally described Curt as a good provider, great father and the love of her life. She noted that he struggled with his guilt and compulsion to have sex with other women. She said that he was now in therapy, AA with a month's sobriety and working hard to make amends. Her biggest concern was with her parents who were demanding she leave him.

I am not in my office to judge Curt but I am there to support Sally. And I won't achieve this by telling her to leave the jerk.

We are instinctual beings endowed with reason and morality, though when an affair takes place the latter two traits may be absent. Our instincts can be manipulated and there are men and women out there who deliberately set out to seduce others for challenge or sport. It is important to know that the psychological technology to achieve this has improved in recent years with the advent of the pickup movement.

Now books, online forums and even training weekends exist dedicated to using evolutionary psychology, neurolinguistic programming and other approaches to the end of having sex with the "target". Maybe you can't cheat an honest man (or woman) but it has become easier to sway the vulnerable or those fantasizing about an adventure in sex or love.

This is the flip side of the aftermath of two people "in love", where they are left wounded and confused. In this scenario there is a betrayed spouse, one who is guilty and feels used and someone who may not feel anything at all as they move on to the next conquest.

It is a pity he did not write in pencil. As you have no doubt frequently observed the impression usually goes through - a fact that has dissolved many a happy marriage.

Arthur Conan Doyle, The Return of Sherlock Holmes

It has become much easier to cheat. No longer the awkward married person trying to hide a ring in a dark bar. Now we have websites dedicated to facilitating every step of the affair. Add to that our electronic devices. No more *"I told you never to call me at the house!"* and hello *"u r so hot when u wear that tie 2 wrk lol"* in the privacy of your cell phone.

All of the above situations provide different challenges but there is one question that is going to drive everyone crazy.

Why did they do it?

"Why" is the question but in most cases it is more accurate to read it as: Why did would you do this to *us*."

Monica started to cry: "We have fabulous sex, a great life, and wonderful kids. I want to understand why you did this."

Colin to Monica: "I really don't know myself."

It is a critical question but difficult to answer because often the cheater doesn't know themselves, the reason is dumb and banal, or woven deeply into their emotional and family history. Good people can do awful things to other good people.

We don't like to believe this; we all think we are good people but there is ample evidence from things as disparate as genocide and workplace mobbing that under the right circumstances people can abandon their moral centre and injure others.

Your cheating spouse may be a sociopathic philanderer but it is more likely that they are a good person who has committed a destructive act. It is the most human of flaws.

Almost every sinful action ever committed can be traced back to a selfish motive. It is a trait we hate in other people but justify in ourselves.

Stephen Kendrick, The Love Dare

I hate the "why" question, though I respect the person asking. It usually comes up and is usually hard to answer. Even when it is answered the betrayed spouse can find the answer unsatisfactory. They understandably think: *In order to have done this to us you must have had a really important reason.*

This means that no answer will measure up. Let me list some reasons I might hear in my office, with the knowledge that they won't measure up.

I wanted to feel desired.

I wanted to have sex with someone else.

I was drunk.

Our marriage hasn't worked for a long time.

I don't know if I love you anymore.

I have felt so alone lately.

He was there when I needed someone.

She said that she needed to have someone touch her, just for one night.

I wanted someone around who was nice to me; that's not you anymore.

I wasn't thinking.

I think someone slipped me a roofie.

I needed to escape you.

I didn't think you would care.

I thought I was in love.

I wanted to get even for the affair you had.

Everybody does this.

We agreed to an open marriage and you are backing out now?

I don't know why I did it.

I often find a kind of dissociation at play. People having affairs seldom take a moment and ask themselves what they are doing, what is driving them, and the impact of their actions on their partner. They are master self deceivers.

When your lover is a liar, you and he have a lot in common; you're both lying to you.

Susan Forward

One of the things that make this so difficult returns to the (slightly reworded) question of: "Why did you do this to *me*?"

Many people who have a transgression committed against them asked themselves first: "Did I do something wrong?" The quick answer is no. You may be a flawed or even terrible spouse but that does not justify an affair.

I am never an absolutist when it comes to the psychological complexities of human beings. While I don't blame the injured party neither do I excuse them from the work of recovery. This is unfair but necessary. Working through issues in the marriage must come secondary to the crisis response.

Take care of your physical health

It's common to reject or punish yourself when you've been rejected by others. When you experience disappointment from the way your family or others treat you, that's the time to take special care of yourself. What are you doing to nurture yourself? What are you doing to protect yourself? Find a healthy way to express your pain.
Christina Enevoldsen

This is always your foundation for moving forward. As obvious as this directive is people under severe stress neglect exercise, sleep, proper nutrition and hydration. They may also engage in addictive behaviors including misuse of alcohol, drugs, food, shopping, sex and gambling. We all have our bad place to go when we are under stress, the place where we can divert or numb our emotions.

I am not one of those who assume you can become a monk at your worst moments. Don't try. Improve your self-care. Recognize your flaws and understand the current need for moderation. Now comes the tricky part. See your health care provider and get tested for STDs. Is this embarrassing, unpleasant and unfair? Yes, yes and yes. Is it necessary? Yes again.

Rick was engaged in an emotional affair with a woman he met online. After he was caught he swore to his wife Chantelle that there had never been physical contact between them. Chantelle said, "You lied about everything else, why should I believe you now?"

So was Rick lying or telling the truth? I have no idea and neither does Chantelle. Even in therapy circumstances can change. People say the affair is over and a few sessions later admit it's not (now I feel cheated on), or someone comes to a marriage counselling session and tells me that the spouse who wasn't having an affair has left to live with the other person.

For most of us if our wife says she stopped at the mall on the way home that is what happened and we believe her. However, if an affair is disclosed every movement and statement are suspect. Sexually transmitted diseases are common. Some can be transmitted despite condom use, though you may not believe him even if he tells you he wore a condom.

Control your emotions

Kirk: *Your ship is compromised, too close to the singularity to survive without assistance, which we are willing to provide.*
Spock: [speaking privately] Captain, what are you doing?
Kirk: Showing them compassion may be the only way to earn peace with Romulus. It's logic, Spock. I thought you'd like that.
Spock: No, not really. Not this time.
Star Trek

More than anything else I see in my office infidelity and its responses are driven by intense and primitive emotions. These emotions must be managed if you are going to survive the crisis. There is likely some explanation for these emotions from the mists of time to do with evolutionary advantage but in the present they can overwhelm normally stable people.

When I am counselling couples I watch both closely to monitor their mental status. To me the risk that one might decompensate is real and I don't want additional dysfunction or even suicide attempts to occur.

I look for genuine displays of distress and feel reassured by them. People *are* distressed and *of course* they should show it, particularly in an environment where it is appropriate (privately, with close friends or relatives, or with a therapist).

Never apologize for showing feeling. When you do you apologize for the truth

Benjamin Disraeli

I tend to be wary of the individual who shows little emotion and wonder when and how the emotions are going to show. If it is the person who had the affair they already have a record of denial. The emotions are overwhelming and frightening but they will not kill you, nor will you permanently lose your sanity.

Spock: I am as conflicted as I once was as a child.
Sarek: You will always be a child of two worlds. I am grateful for this, and for you.
Spock: I feel anger for the one who took Mother's life - an anger I cannot control.
Sarek: I believe... that she would say, "Do not try to."
Star Trek

Someone who is having an ongoing affair has time to think about what they are doing. They may contemplate a disclosure, being caught or what their spouse might say. They might be thinking about leaving their spouse. In other words the clock has started on integrating the information that needs to be processed. That this information is often clouded with self deceit doesn't change the fact that *at least they know what is going on.*

The spouse in the dark has no time at all. This is an important consideration since their clock will only start ticking for them once they find out. They may think they have a great marriage or they may be wondering why sex has fallen off or why their partner seems so furtive and distracted.

Moreover, once the disclosure occurs they will be looking for a time frame: *"How long has this been going on?"* Once that has been established (let's say a year) the question becomes: *"So has our life together, our lovemaking, and our conversations all been lies for the past year?"*

People who have been cheated on usually (though . always) have questions; lots and lots of questions. The often want to know everything about that time frame.

Rita discovered that Andy had been having an affair for the past year with a woman he met online. She became fixated on questions and details. Andy thought he was going to go mad answering them and endlessly going over what happened. In particular Rita wanted to know if his affair had been sexual at the time of their stay at a Bed and Breakfast on their Anniversary. In her mind it had been a wonderful and loving weekend. But she really needed to know what to do with that memory. Despite his insistence that it was not sexual at that time and that their Anniversary weekend was wonderful for him too, Rita kept asking.

Rage

"The truth will set you free, but first it will piss you off."

Gloria Steinem

It means something more than anger. It is an intense emotion that feels overwhelming and out of control. It is difficult if not impossible to hide. It is fed by thoughts of hurt, betrayal and injustice. Chinese medicine sees rage burning you up from the inside. Turned inward it can cause sickness, even death. Outwards, it can be turned against loved ones or people unlucky enough to cross your path at the wrong moment.

Sometimes betrayed spouses fantasize about violent acts; thoughts that are often disturbing in individuals who are normally peaceful and loving. I have some suggestions for addressing rage.

You have good reason to be angry. You may be getting the message everywhere that something is wrong with your emotions but anger - an emotion meant to address violated boundaries - is congruent and appropriate.

Recognize that fantasy is just that - fantasy. Having a fantasy does not mean you will act on it. It is rare for someone who has not previously been violent to become violent. If you do have thoughts of acting on your anger get help.

Sit down and acknowledge to yourself that acts of rage injure you further. This is part of being self aware of your thoughts and emotions.

Find a trusted person that you can use as a reality check. In other words keep a source of perspective close by. Let them tell you when your rage is out of line.

Suicidal Thoughts

The idea of taking your own life is about as extreme as it gets. In bad moments people may wonder if the world would be better off without them. Outside of the current situation - pay attention - you are a unique and loved individual. You have options and this feeling is temporary. You can and will heal. I'm not saying that it's easy; I'm just saying that you can do it.

If you are feeling suicidal here are some practical measures you can take:

First, if these are just passing thoughts remember that many people have them for all kinds of reasons. Having thoughts is not the same as acting on them. They are disturbing but don't make you strange, they are a sign that it's time to make some changes.

Find someone trustworthy like friend, spiritual advisor or therapist. Tell them about these feelings and come up with a plan should they get out of hand (meaning that you are seriously considering acting on them). Do not swear them to secrecy; instead tell them that if should they ever believe you are going to act on these thoughts to do everything in their power to stop you.

Make and carry a list of people or places you can call at any time. Include a local crisis number and the location of the nearest emergency ward.

Seek professional help. I don't think all our problems need professional helpers but I do for this. Doctors, social workers, and psychologists should neither be shocked nor deterred by someone's suicidal feelings. Their job is to get you to help or come up with a plan. If you feel ignored after you have expressed your concerns move on to someone else.

You have options. You always have options. Anything can be recreated, except your life.

Do I ever use guilt in these situations? You betcha. You think people would be better off without you? Think again - those who care about you would be devastated and terribly injured by your loss.

The world is full of wonders, good and loving people. Maybe you screwed up royally or your cherished values have been violated. But it's not time to take a life; it's time to build a new one.

Managing your emotions

This topic is a separate book but remember, we have the technology. Intense emotions have always been with us and at different times in history they were more or less accepted. This concept is to a certain extent culture bound and perceived differently in men and women. It is important to remember with few exceptions that *we all feel*. It is not unusual for someone to say to me: *"Oh, she is fine with this. I'm falling apart and she's not affected."* So back to the hundred pound brick.

At the writing of this book there are literally hundreds of approaches to therapy, spiritual communities that embrace healing and prayer, energy and neurological approaches that can help someone begin to relax and heal.

Remember that anyone under stress has primitive vigilance responses placing them in a state of high physiological arousal. This contributes to emotional suffering and can make you sick over time. I am a hypnotherapist and use self hypnosis. There is also a local acupuncturist I go to see who uses the needles to *"...quiet your body, Richard."* People in my business under strain often throw the kitchen sink at the problem.

There is much out there to help you. Again, ask around; these things often cost money and there are a few quacks. But don't limit yourself. Much can be accomplished outside the box.

Narrative

We define our lives with stories. We carry narratives in our head and words. Be aware of your narrative. For example:

He cheated on me and this is the end of everything I value. I will never again trust the same way and never again feel completely safe in a relationship.

And

I have always loved him but he has been such a fool and look at him now. This is the hardest thing we have been through as a couple but maybe with hard work we can make things work together.

The two narratives above could easily be about the same situation. And both are likely true. One, however, is going to inspire frustration and a degree of hopelessness. The language is catastrophic. The second statement allows for the challenge of the situation, is forward looking and leaves room for growth.

Intrusive thoughts

No matter the struggle - affairs or otherwise - people come to me and say they can't get the thoughts out of their heads. These thoughts intrude on recreation, work and sleep. They are distressing and tend to gravitate towards terrible scenarios. In my practise I tend to go one of two ways with this issue (just me, there are many ways of addressing anything). I may use a mindfulness reframe.

Remember that these thoughts are the way your unconscious mind processes the grief. They will not hurt you or go on forever. If you want you can use the mantra, "your thoughts go by as clouds" to distance them.

Sometimes I use CBT (Cognitive Behavioral Therapy) techniques. For example there are a number of structured formats in Cognitive Therapy that allow people to sit down and organize their thoughts, examine the evidence for them and frame them in an accurate but manageable format.

I like to use a snap band on myself. This sophisticated piece of technological treatment involves placing an elastic band around your wrist and snapping it when thoughts intrude. The last time my grandson had heart surgery I used one to catch and extinguish intrusive catastrophic thoughts.

One of the biggest tricks to managing difficult emotions is to flow into them instead of away from them. Be proactive; make yourself the client, patient or experimental subject. You have a problem to solve; go after it with gusto.

Past, and other troubles

Someone has had an affair, or you have. You may have had (or have) other troubles in life. The affair or disclosure of the affair may compound the emotional past or existing issues. Think of the doctor treating a sudden heart problem who needs to know that you are diabetic. I might hear from my clients:

"I was raised by an alcoholic parent."

"I am being treated for cancer."

"I am a recovering drug addict."

"I have been hospitalized in the past for severe anxiety."

"We were in a car accident a year ago."

"My mother just died."

"My father had multiple affairs."

"My ex wife cheated on me."

"Our son is autistic."

"I have had episodes of depression."

This is just a short list of things that may be relevant, compounded or exacerbated by an affair.

The affair ends now

This means everything; all contact, texts, email, calls and involvement. This can be a challenge, particularly when both parties share a workplace. I am never an absolutist on rules. I think life is too complicated for me to say this *has* to be. Still, this is an important principle.

Jill had an affair with her co-worker, Jamie. They were a successful sales team at work, which ensured financial and professional success. They worked together and were on the road together. Jill's husband demanded she leave her job right away. Jill countered with: "But the affair is over and our finances depend on my continuing to make good money."

Similarly,

Every summer Anne and Kyle participated in a local road rally group. They were constantly planning social events and rallies, even during the off season. It was fun and kept them involved with a large social group. When it turned out that Kyle was sleeping with Tracey, another woman in the group, Anne immediately left the group. Kyle did too but they were left answering embarrassing questions from concerned friends, particularly Tracey's confused husband. They stayed together but with a large gap in their lives. In addition to the affair Anne blamed Kyle for ruining their social life and forcing her to lie to Tracey's husband.

These are challenging dilemmas. I often see people trying to get transferred, sending out resumes, quitting social groups or otherwise trying to reduce the harm of contact. The spouse who has been cheated on is almost always deeply uncomfortable with any involvement between their spouse and the other person. There is even a more uncomfortable scenario

Darren worked in a lab with Mark. When Darren's wife disclosed an ongoing affair with Mark day to day work suddenly became an awkward nightmare for Darren.

Less challenging is the casual contact that people sometimes want to maintain ("it's just the occasional text"). Stop it. Now.

I have some sympathy for the cheater. She's attached. She made love to this guy and while saying goodbye forever is the right thing to do it is still wrenching. And the other person will be hurting too. You may have to go back to your spouse and completely forsake the other but now you have managed to wound two people.

Get some help

Star Trek

This can take a few forms, including reading about infidelity or seeing a counselor. You might also need to see someone if you are having violent or suicidal thoughts. Having someone objective and knowledgeable is important while emotions are out of control. There are risks and possible consequences to telling friends and family.

If you see a counsellor or therapist as a couple, or as an individual, there are professional restraints in place; including confidentiality. Most of us are going to allow clients to explore and manage their emotions, not add fuel to the fire. We are aware that becoming locked into anger is destructive and that you will go through phases of recovery.

Also, most therapists are not absolute in their pronouncements. We tentatively explore people's options to help them make choices that are right for them.

Marriage counselling is an activity that requires skill and as I have mentioned, not all therapists have those skills or are interested in obtaining them. Therapy can be expensive. Much is at stake but believe me when I say that whatever we charge most of us come in well under lawyer fees. In most jurisdictions there are a few places people can look.

Many employees are covered under Employee Assistance Plans (EAP). They provide counselling to employees through a third party organization as part of their benefits plan. Counselling tends to be responsive, good quality, though short term in nature. Most EAP therapists do quite a bit of marital work and are experienced with issues surrounding infidelity. EAP providers place a high value on confidentiality so employees feel safe in accessing them.

Many religious communities place high value on the importance of marriage and have people available to members to help them in a crisis.

Moderate sized towns and cities often have family service organizations which provide counselling services to the community; typically on a sliding scale of fees.

Most communities have private practitioners who will see you for a fee. Some of these fees may be covered under insurance plans.

Professional Associations and Colleges often have referral services that will identify qualified people in your community.

The majority of therapists who deliver marital counselling will have Masters Degrees in Social Work, Psychology, or Counselling, or belong to a discipline that has a counselling sub specialty (Education, Nursing, Medicine, Divinity, Occupational therapy). Some practitioners at the Doctoral level (mainly Psychology) will offer marital counselling. Ask around. Do you know someone who has seen a marital counsellor? Do you have a professional friend or family doctor who can recommend someone?

Counselling is personal. It is art, craft and science. There are well recognized things that make it work:

The reading and work you both do outside of the session. This is important because healing involves work.

You both feel comfortable and engaged with the counsellor. Building rapport is job one for a therapist; it is the art of therapy. The therapist must convey that they understand who created this situation but also that they have compassion and responsibility towards both of you. This is important for the times when therapists have to be blunt and push you into challenging territory.

There must be, somewhere, the quality of hope. Some kind of memory of what you can bring to each other, desire to change or opportunity for moving forward. Good therapists convey optimism about the capacity of human beings to address and overcome challenges in their lives.

No rash actions

Decisions to walk out, confront the other party, have a payback affair, or put the house on the market will likely end badly. Neither of you are at your best right now; any decisions you make will be distorted by extreme emotion. We think of ourselves as being rational, but in the grips of extreme emotion we really are not. Everyone is prone to doing dumb things when filled with sadness, confusion and rage. People have tunnel vision and lack perspective.

For couples coping with infidelity their spouse, home, every word, and touch are reminders of pain. This is where a therapist, member of the clergy, level headed friend or family member can be useful. You will likely need someone who can say. *"Hey, not yet"* (family member), *"Have you thought about some of the implications of this decision?"* (therapist) or *"Are you nuts, bro?"* (friend).

Allow yourselves time

Patience and time do more than strength or passion.
Jean de La Fontaine

Psychological blows take time to heal. They cannot be rushed. This is not going to be better in four weeks or even four months. It may get better then worse again. Everyone will go through stages of grief. You will never forget what happened; that innocence is gone forever, but you may be able to move forward and make your marriage better. This concept is extraordinarily difficult for people in distress to grasp.

They imagine being in the same state of distress forever and it can panic them. They really won't but fear it nonetheless. Every time something triggers emotion, it feels like the wound reopens.

Therapists understand the challenges of time and the feeling of being stuck that some people experience. Family and friends may not *("hey, just let it go")*.

Typically, the cheating spouse is looking forward to the day when this is off the table and the other person is wondering if it will ever stop. They often tell me that the affair is never out of their head. This can put a great deal of pressure on both parties.

I often compare grieving with a broken limb in a cast. You can get medical help, care for the limb but nothing is going to heal it faster under that cast and when the cast is off the limb will be withered and weak, entailing the need for rehabilitation.

The person who had the affair takes responsibility.

> *It was your choice to sleep with her Gavin!*
> *It didn't just happen!*
> *Belinda G. Buchanan*

Maybe you were having marital problems and maybe they will have to be addressed. That never excuses an affair and doesn't matter in the short run. If the person who had the affair does not take full responsibility then the marriage will not recover.

This is a straightforward idea that has some complexity behind it. It is as close as I get to an "absolute". No one can make someone else have an affair. And there are many troubled marriages where people do not cheat. And, as hard as it is for some, people can survive without sex.

There are two better responses to a troubled marriage. One is using the resources available to heal troubled marriages. We know a lot about common communication and emotional struggles, and how to manage them. Dr. John Gottman, for example, has gone to extraordinary lengths as a researcher and clinician to understand and find ways of making marriages better.

The other alternative is to leave. If your marriage is so anguished that you believe an affair is needed or you have no hope that it can improve then maybe you should consider separation or divorce.

Jane and Brent had struggled in their marriage for years, with bitter arguments, no sexual intimacy and many unresolved issues. So Brent was surprised that Jane fell to pieces after he had an affair. "Surely this was inevitable?" he said in therapy. "How can you cheat on a dead marriage?" Jane countered: "I always held on to the hope that we could work things out."

Or

The second time Joan's husband cheated she realized that she had no feelings left, or hope that he could ever change. She had suffered so much from his cheating and marriage counselling had been useless. She went online and started searching for an apartment.

I find that things can become confusing if we are trying to address the emotional crisis following the disclosure of infidelity and trying to sort out what was wrong with the marriage at the same time. It can imply that one problem caused the other and therefore invalidates the emotions of the person facing the shock of discovery.

I prefer to manage the crisis to the point where both parties feel ready to address the marital issues and then move onto the deeper problems.

The person who cheated enters a period of transparency

This is another tricky rule to be absolute in execution, though the principles reflect a psychological truth. Without trust every move by the cheating spouse is questioned. That means every text, email, call and moment away are suspect, let alone a night in a hotel room out of town. This can be maddening to both spouses. One is tormented by doubt and suspicion and the other has their every move scrutinized.

The difficulty of transparency becomes apparent with spouses of soldiers (away on training or deployment), police officers (communication by phone at odd hours) or therapists (confidential communication with colleagues and clients).

Come as close as you can. This may mean surrendering passwords, Visa bills, or phone records. It may mean three calls a night when on the road. It means talking about things that other couples take for granted. It doesn't mean harassment, stalking, hidden cameras or things that truly invade personal space. There are some grey areas but we are trying to restore a marriage to health and equity, not escalate punishment. This will only be helpful as a temporary measure.

There is never a reason for abusive behavior

There's going to be anger and rage that needs to be expressed. Deep and powerful emotions that feel (but are not) out of control. Abuse and degradation will wound not heal and could add legal trouble to an already volatile situation. If you believe you cannot control your words or behaviors seek out professional help for anger management. It won't feel fair if your spouse has cheated but the job is healing, not compounding problems. So how do you express your anger?

Throwing things, name calling, destroying personal items, getting in someone's personal space, mistreating pets, pounding walls, making threats and screaming are intimidating and experienced as abusive. And certainly shoves, blows or other forced or violent contact.

As difficult as it is I recommend that you do your best to be temperate in your language. Consider one of *"The Four Agreements"* based on the book by Don Miguel Ruiz. This book has helped many people and suggests when you are "immaculate with your word" you understand words as white magic or black magic. This means your words can be healing and positive ("We will get through this if we work together.") or destructive and negative ("We are losers and deserve to be apart.")

In addition the narrative in your head can be positive ("I have the strength to get through this.") or negative ("I have screwed up everything."). If you become self aware you will understand the story we ascribe to our life has tremendous power over ourselves and others. This does not suggest spin or self deception. It does suggest we can be realistic and positive at the same time.

Be careful with whom you share information

> *People are always fascinated by infidelity because, in the end - whether we've had direct experience or not - there's part of you that knows there's absolutely no more piercing betrayal. People are undone by it.*
> *Junot Diaz*

Experts in trauma will tell you that in the aftermath of a shock people may be traumatically open or closed. Picture the survivor of a fire who is either sitting with his arms wrapped around himself, silent and withdrawn, or, conversely, babbling. People who find out about the affair will always remember. I am not saying to tell no one but to think through the implications of telling certain people. While some people are clear they don't want anyone to know, few want to be alone with the hurt.

They are human, want support and their confidantes around them. I can understand this but close friends and family members are going to have opinions that might become problematic later.

Friends and family care about you and judge those who hurt you. They experience anger towards the cheating spouse. They may become angry and take it on themselves to speak to the cheater. They want to stand up for you and protect you. There is nothing wrong with this but when you are ready to move forward in your marriage it can become a problem.

Mario had gone through a period of massive shock after he found out about Tammy's affair. He had told his friends and family that she had an affair with a man in a city where her company had a branch office. They attended counselling, talked extensively then decided to renew their vows and move forward. That's when Mario found that his parents refused to allow Tammy back in their house. He was close to his parents and now he felt torn. Tammy, who had previously been close to her mother in law felt wounded and lost.

Sometimes a confidante blames the victim or provides unhelpful advice.

Rob turned to his best friend after his wife had a one night stand. He was reeling and deeply saddened. His buddy said, "You have never worn the pants in the family man, what do you expect? I'm going to take you out on Saturday and you are going to have your own one night stand."

There are those who want to broadcast the mendacity of their spouse to the world; making sure that friends and family know. They feel punitive and sometimes want to degrade someone as they feel degraded. Punishing responses are not healing responses; they will build further walls to emotional recovery, even where the marriage is going to end.

This brings us to one of the most difficult issues that can arise.

Penny never dreamed that Jon would have an affair. Her first response was rage. She tracked down the husband of Jon's lover and arranged to meet him for coffee and tell him his wife was a cheat. When she saw the hurt and confusion on his face she realized that she had made a mistake.

There are unforeseen consequences to intimate information getting out that isn't seen in advance or controlled.

Dave, a police officer, wanted to tell his wife's lover exactly what he thought of a man who would seduce another man's wife. So he went to his house and confronted him. Though he was not threatening or in uniform, the other man called Dave's Staff Sergeant and complained. Dave was subsequently disciplined.

Strengths

People under stress often overlook their strengths. They may be competent at work, great problem solvers, devoted parents and friends, and even their marriage may have many strengths. This is important to understand during any process of change or healing. These abilities not totally separate. You may go through moments of great despair but in the end your strengths are going to matter.

Carrie was a project manager with a large staff and a record of achievement. She had devoted friends and had supported her daughter through a sexual assault. When her husband cheated she told me, "I have never felt so helpless".

I told her the feeling was understandable but she was certainly not helpless.

People in crisis seldom realize the skills used to solve one set of problems can be applied to others in different realms.

Carrie set to work reading the literature on infidelity. She spoke to a friend who was a lawyer, joined a gym and started on a CBT workbook to help manage her emotions. This did not make the problem go away but put her in a stronger position to address it.

Carrie is not a therapist but she has many skills. She will go through all the predictable struggles associated with the disclosure of an affair but she will go through them with agency (the ability to influence events) and communion (her social supports).

Sex

> *Good sex is like good bridge. If you don't have a good partner, you'd better have a good hand.*
> Mae West

With sex you have primitive emotions compounding primitive emotions. And to counsel couples for infidelity is to see instinct at its strongest. I don't try to stop the rushing river. In some couples the intuitive thing happens. In my mind it means no sex until the STD test results are in and someone feels safe enough for intimacy again. Just as often I see couples having intense and frequent sexual contact in the weeks following the disclosure.

Sandra told me, "I have no idea why I'm even touching him, but we are having sex almost every day. And it's great sex."

I don't judge this (aside from raising concerns about STD's) but I do ask people to consider what is going on in their emotions.

We were having sex and I found myself wondering: Did he touch her like that? Did she give him oral sex? Did they ever have sex at our house in our bed? I suddenly wanted to run out of the bedroom.

I also point out that like most grief experiences things can change quickly and no matter how much sex they are having the recovery is going to take more time than they expect. In fact, a common response I witness to any relaxation of vigilance (which might just be a pleasant dinner together) is a sudden return of the fear response.

Jerry told me that they were having a nice afternoon and when he came back from the kitchen she was withdrawn and angry.

What I do say strongly is that everyone feel in control of their bodies. In other words, if either party does not want sex it is a decision to be immediately accepted. Sex is a powerful intimate act and will need to be discussed in or out of therapy.

Improving your marriage

This is a book on the emergency response to disclosure of an affair, not a book about improving your marriage. Think of the emergency room where bleeding has to be staunched and the patient stabilized before the deeper illness is diagnosed and addressed.

Marriages struggle and fail for many reasons; some more serious than others. A couple goes through developmental changes together over the life of their marriage. These include the arrival of children, the challenges of the teen years, kids leaving the home, loss of parents, arrival of grandchildren, retirement and death of a partner.

Many of the problems I see in my office are related to difficulties linked to these stages. In addition the stress of modern life can make an extra crisis (a sick child) or an unexpected one (job loss) overwhelming. It is common for me to see two good people contemplating separation because of their failure to pull together during stress.

The presence of an affair is not an indication of gravity of the marriage problems. People have affairs in pretty good marriages and in terrible ones too. Serious problems can involve abuse, addiction and mental illness. Where these problems are present an individual in the marriage is going to need professional help to address emotions and behaviors. They can destroy a marriage as easily as an affair.

There are many ways to heal and counselling is just one among many. But I also have a surpassing belief that healing is possible and with understanding and work most couples can find a way to move forward.

There is no formula for marriage counselling. I find that it starts with a commitment to move forward then lots of work. I draw on teachings from CBT, my work with the unconscious mind, Brief Solution Focused therapy, Systemic Family therapy and the works of Dr. John Gottman. And anything else that pops into my head, including the most profound advice for any marriage (including mine), *"recognize the stupid things you say and stop saying them."*

The Kids

Kids are highly sensitive to their parents, and environment; no matter their age. You are upset, bewildered or angry and they can feel it on some level. Young children won't understand the nature of infidelity, most teenagers and young adults will understand the basics all too well. No matter what happens between parents the crisis of infidelity remains a family crisis.

This is complicated by the fact that kids vary considerably in maturity and cognitive skills so in the end parents need to know their kids well enough to know what to say. This could range from a frank conversation with a young adult to extra soothing for a toddler. As I've said people can be traumatically closed ("Why is mommy sleeping all the time?") or open ("Your daddy loves another woman more than me.").

It is important to carefully craft a message to your kids, preferably from both of you. Depending on what they know or you have told them, prepare to be judged. Your kids are not therapists, diplomats or necessarily nuanced. You are their parents and they will have opinions which may not be accurate or politically correct. (*"Maybe if you had been nicer to Dad he wouldn't have had to go elsewhere."*).

They may not express opinions but express them in other ways:

"Son, are you using a condom with that girl?"

"Are you?"

Or

"The school called today, they found drugs in Dakota's locker."

Never forget that the affair affects everyone around you.

After the affair Charles's 28 year old son refused to even talk to him. His wife had to intervene and tell him to lighten up and let them get on with their healing.

Some kids will think it's their fault. For many parents the presence of kids will either escalate the guilt or provide inventive for renewed healing.

Forgiveness

> *To forgive is to set a prisoner free and discover*
> *that the prisoner was you.*
> *Lewis B Smedes*

You have discovered that the person you trusted the most has betrayed your trust. What follows include sleepless nights, panic attacks, searing emotional pain, obsession, cognitive distortions, and in the worst cases, suicidal thoughts or physical illness. Forgiveness is the gold standard of healing but how do you forgive the people who create this desolation?

I have witnessed rape victims pressured to forgive unrepentant rapists and move on. I have talked to men who beat their wives for the affirmation that eventual forgiveness provided them. I have seen people wield forgiveness like personal power to provide absolution. And expressions like, "forgive and forget" seem more applicable to neglecting a birthday than the terrible things people do to each other.

It will never be easy or quick. But what is the alternative to forgiveness? Holding on to hate, anger, thoughts of vengeance? While anger can serve a temporary purpose, inspiring you to protect yourself and others, hate and vengeance are the antithesis of healing.

Forgiveness is not necessarily reconciliation, though it would be part of a reconciliation process. If the marriage is to be saved it will involve remorse by the cheater but if the marriage fails, not necessarily. *In the end it is a process of letting go and moving on.*

Do your healing, and some day, when you are ready, close that door and come back fully to the world where you are loved and cherished for the special person you were meant to be.

Kim and Barrie's story

Kim and Barrie were under stress. They both had challenging jobs, two young children and problems with communication. In addition Barrie's father was struggling with cancer. Though only married five years they had forgotten how much they loved each other at the beginning. Their lives felt like a big "to do" list. Barrie was out of shape and depressed, while Kim worked out constantly.

When Kevin came to work in Kim's office he struck everyone as charming and fun. He knew how to engage people and seemed to genuinely care about his colleagues. He was married but seldom mentioned his wife. He made Kim laugh and jokingly let her know how attractive he found her.

Kim had not felt appreciated in some time, nor had she felt much by way of fun and laughter. Kevin was like a breath of fresh air. She looked forward to going to work and dreaded coming home to her frustrated and angry husband. She and Kevin started to text each other in joking and flirtatious ways. She even went as far as to send him a picture of her topless.

One night while they were alone in the office they shared a deep and passionate kiss. Kim wrapped her arms around him then Kevin put his hand on her breast but stepped back when he felt her stiffen. Kim was flustered and sexually aroused. She made an excuse and left the office. Kevin texted her saying it felt good to touch and kiss her. He was starting to care about her deeply.

When Kim arrived home she ran into the bedroom; saying nothing to Barrie. He tried to approach her but she was clearly upset. He was worried and wondering what to do when he heard her phone beep. Thinking that something had happened he picked it up and read the text from Kevin.

After Barrie finished reading all the texts he walked into the bedroom, tossed her phone on the bed and said, "You got a text from Kevin. I'll be on the couch tonight."

Kim was humiliated. She didn't know what to say and in the morning quietly went to work. There she ran into Kevin. He tried to speak to her but she was so confused and shamed that she just walked away from that conversation.

She could barely face going home at the end of the day but when she did the kids were at their grandparents and Barrie was waiting for her. It was clear that he had been crying.

"I know it's been hard," he said, "but did you have to do this to us? I would have gone for marriage counselling. Now it's over."

Kim panicked. She tried to apologise but it just came out as stammering and tears. She was consumed by guilt, shame and humiliation. Barrie continued:

"You have never sent me pictures like that and now that guy has them and is going to do God knows what with them. What were you thinking? This has been hard but I thought we were going through it together. I need you to stay away from me while I think."

The weeks that followed were challenging for both of them. Barrie's father took a turn for the worse, while all Barrie could do was think about what happened with Kim. He almost called Kevin from his office but a colleague grabbed the phone from him and told him he should call a marriage counsellor. He lost ten pounds, became increasingly depressed and constantly pestered Kim with questions. He did not believe there had never been sex between them outside of the kiss. He went to his doctor and was tested for STD's. His doctor also put him on an anti-depressant.

Kim was beside herself and couldn't escape the constant sense of shame. She hated herself for hurting Barrie, couldn't even look at Kevin and had moments where she felt suicidal. Kevin had started to ignore her at the office and she desperately wanted to ask him what he was going to do with the photograph. One day a colleague told her that a slightly edited version of the photograph had turned up on Kevin's Facebook page. Kim broke down.

Family life was a nightmare. The frightened kids were needy and demanding, trying to get reassurance from their parents. Kim and Barrie had never needed each other more - even a touch from Kim made Barrie jump - and it was all they could do to work out a grocery list.

So a month after the disclosure Kevin remembered his colleagues' advice and called an EAP company to make an appointment for counselling. Walking into that office felt like one of the most difficult things they had ever done.

Anita, the counsellor put them immediately at their ease. Neither of them had ever been to counselling before and had no idea what to expect. Barrie was worried that a female counsellor would try to justify Kim's affair based on his failure as a husband. Kim was worried that she would be judged and debased in front of her husband.

Neither of those things happened. Anita's immediate concern was to help them manage the emotional crisis and ensure that they were taking care of their health. She also wanted to know if Kim was still in contact with Kevin and the direction they wanted to take in their marriage. Kim was surprised; her fantasy was that Anita would tell

Barrie to leave her and she desperately did not want that to happen. She was hugely relieved when he told her that he wanted to somehow make this work.

The months ahead were difficult. Barrie's father died and his mother who had figured out what had happened shunned Kim at the funeral. Kevin's wife phoned Kim at work asking why he had that picture on Facebook. However, the counselling provided some structure for understanding what happened and lots of homework from Anita. They began to talk outside of sessions and resumed the sexual part of their relationship.

After a month of therapy Anita started to introduce communication exercises into the sessions, along with suggestions for reading materials. She insisted that as difficult as this situation was their marriage had many strengths and this represented an opportunity for them to move forward better than before.

Barrie kept pressure on Kim to quit her job; saying Kevin was a toxic influence and she needed to be away from him. Kim agreed but countered that they had to pay the mortgage. This pressure was relieved when Kevin found work elsewhere. Kim still felt embarrassed at work but stayed.

A year later the memories remained but life carried on normally. Both Kim and Barrie believed they could eventually get beyond the pain. They were more open with each other about emotions. They talked every day, made time to be together and enjoyed each other's company.

Final thoughts

> *What greater thing is there for two human souls, than*
> *to feel that they are joined for life - to strengthen each*
> *other in all labor, to rest on each other in all sorrow, to*
> *minister to each other in all pain, to be one with each*
> *other in silent unspeakable memories at the moment of*
> *the last parting?*
> *George Eliot, Adam Bede*

I have been a therapist more than thirty years and had the opportunity to see people at their appalling worst. I also have seen people carry on following trauma, loss and disaster. My work has not made me cynical, quite the opposite. I don't know you so I can't say your marriage will survive this blow. Maybe it is time to leave. What I do know is that working together people can transcend almost any crisis. Hope itself is not folly; it is the animating dynamic behind change. And kindness and laughter are two of the most powerful healing tools in the universe.

Great Resources

This is a list of resources I have used. It is a short list; there are many good books and programs out there for you to find.

Spring, Janis A, After the Affair: Healing the Pain and Rebuilding Trust When a Partner Has Been Unfaithful Harper Collins Publishers, 2012

This is an excellent book and I highly recommend it for a deeper look at the emotional issues surrounding infidelity. Many people have turned to it. If my book is the emergency room, After the Affair is a deeper treatment.

Burns, David D, Feeling Good Together: The Secret to Making Troubled Relationships Work Broadway Books, 2008

Dr. David Burns in an engaging writer with a deep knowledge of Cognitive Behavioral Therapy (CBT). CBT is more understood as an excellent approach for mood issues but is less understood for its utility in helping couples.

Burns, Dr. David D. Feeling Good: The New Mood Therapy, HarperCollins Publishers, 1980

Mood issues are regularly found in conjunction with marital issues. They often need to be acknowledged and addressed separately. This book is a great start.

Chapman, Gary D, the Five Love Languages: How to Express Heartfelt Commitment to Your Mate Thorndike Press, 2005

This book is not a thick tome but a short and practical schema for improving communication and connection with your spouse. It is fun, straightforward and used wisely can result in an immediate improvement in your marriage.

Ruiz, Don Miguel; the Four Agreements, a Practical Guide to Personal

Freedom, Amber-Allen Publishing, 2008

Ruiz loses a few people in the first chapter when he talks about Toltec wisdom but hang in, this is one book I want everyone to read.

Gray, John, Men Are from Mars, Women Are from Venus: Practical Guide for Improving Communication and Getting What You Want in Your Relationships Harper Collins, Apr 23, 1993

According to evolutionary psychology men and woman don't see the world the same. Who knew? Turns out that John Gray pointed this out twenty years ago. Still valuable and worth reading today.

Greenberger, Dr. Dennis, Padesky, Dr. Christine, Mind over Mood: Change

How You Feel by Changing the Way You Think, the Guilford Press, 1995.

This is a time tested classic.

Pittman, Frank S. Private Lies: Infidelity and the Betrayal of Intimacy Norton, 1990

The late Frank Pittman was perhaps the most pragmatic, funny and skilled psychiatrist/ writer of his day. His funny, moral and insightful book on affairs remains a must read for those who have been effected by an affair in any way.

Gottman, John; Seven principles for making marriage work: A Practical

Guide from the Country's Foremost Relationship Expert, Random

House/Three Rivers, 2000

Best guide I have read; very helpful. Even better, Gottman has YouTube videos where he reveals himself to be a funny and engaging speaker. I often ask couples to go home and check them out.

Thanks

There is no question that this book was written with the help of my clients. Those who cheated on their spouses and those who were betrayed. I can neither tell their specific stories nor their names. However, they are brave people who came into the office of someone they didn't know, entrusted him with their worst moment and had the hope and transparency to search for something better. I have deep respect for their choice to move forward.

I have had many teachers in my life, clinical and otherwise. I am a product of their influence. In this book let me single out the late Dr. Vince Caccamo for his wise guidance over many years.

My wife Nina is always the source of my belief in the value and joy of marriage

Printed in Great Britain
by Amazon

55974262R00045